Empower Your Finances

A Smart Spending Guide

RILEY MORGAN

Copyright

© 2024, by Riley Morgan. All rights reserved. No part of this book may be reproduced, stored in a retrieval system, or transmitted in any form or by any means, electronic, mechanical, photocopying, recording, or otherwise, without the prior written permission of the publisher, except for the use of short quotations in a book review.

TABLE OF CONTENTS

Introduction
Chapter 1: The Financial Landscape of 2025
Chapter 2: Assessing Your Financial Health
Chapter 3: Crafting a Flexible Budget
Chapter 4: Building Smart Spending Habits
Chapter 5: The Importance of Saving and Investing
Chapter 6: Mastering Debt Management
Chapter 7: The Importance of Insurance
Chapter 8: The Importance of Estate Planning
Chapter 9: The Importance of Continuous Financial Education
Chapter 10: Travel and Experience Budgeting
Chapter 11: Adapting to Economic Shifts
Chapter 12: Resources for Financial Success
Conclusion

Introduction

In today's rapidly changing economic landscape, understanding how to manage your finances is more important than ever. As we approach 2025, many people find themselves grappling with new financial realities from inflation and rising costs to the increasing influence of digital currencies. This book aims to equip you with the knowledge and tools necessary to navigate these challenges and achieve financial freedom.

Throughout this guide, you will discover practical strategies for budgeting, saving, investing, and spending wisely. Each chapter is designed to provide actionable insights, real-life success stories, and tools that can help you take control of your financial future. Whether you're starting your financial journey or looking to refine your existing strategies, this book is your roadmap to smart spending in 2025.

Chapter 1: The Financial Landscape of 2025

As we approach 2025, understanding the evolving financial landscape is crucial for making informed decisions about spending, saving, and investing. This chapter examines key economic trends and their implications for personal finance, providing you with the insights needed to navigate this new environment effectively.

Key Economic Trends

1. Rising Inflation

Current Context: Inflation rates have fluctuated significantly in recent years, influenced by factors such as the COVID-19 pandemic, supply chain disruptions, and government stimulus measures. As of 2025, inflation is projected to stabilise at a higher baseline than pre-pandemic levels, with estimates ranging from 3% to 5% annually.

Impact on Purchasing Power: This inflationary environment means that the purchasing power of your dollar is diminishing. For instance, if your grocery bill was $100 in 2020, it might rise to $110–$115 in 2025 for the same items.

Strategies for Consumers

Budget Adjustments: Re-evaluate your budget to accommodate rising costs. Consider increasing allocations for essential categories like food and utilities.

Smart Shopping: Utilise tools such as price comparison apps and loyalty programs to find the best deals. Buying in bulk or during sales can also help mitigate costs.

Investing in Assets: Consider investing in assets that historically outpace inflation, such as real estate or commodities like gold.

2. Digital Currencies

Emerging Landscape: The rise of cryptocurrencies continues to reshape the financial landscape. Major players like Bitcoin and Ethereum have gained traction, while countries explore central bank digital currencies (CBDCs). For example, the U.S. Federal Reserve is actively researching the implementation of a digital dollar.

Benefits and Risks:

Advantages: Digital currencies offer faster transaction speeds and lower fees compared to traditional banking systems. They can also provide a hedge against inflation if properly invested.

Risks: The volatility of cryptocurrencies can lead to significant financial losses. For instance, Bitcoin has experienced fluctuations from $20,000 to over $60,000 within a year.

Practical Steps:

Education: Familiarise yourself with how cryptocurrencies work, including blockchain technology, wallets, and exchanges.

Investment Caution: If considering cryptocurrency investments, start with a small percentage of your portfolio and diversify across different assets.

3. Sustainability and Ethical Spending

Consumer Awareness: A growing number of consumers are prioritising sustainability in their purchasing decisions. According to a 2023 survey by Nielsen, 73% of millennials are willing to pay more for sustainable brands.

Shifting Market Dynamics: Companies that demonstrate a commitment to ethical practices, such as using eco-friendly materials or fair labour practices, are experiencing increased consumer loyalty. Brands like Patagonia and Tesla have set benchmarks in this area.

Practical Steps for Consumers:
Research Brands: Use websites like Good On You to evaluate the ethical practices of brands before making purchases.

Support Local: Whenever possible, support local businesses and farmers, which can reduce your carbon footprint and stimulate the local economy.

4. Remote Work and the Gig Economy

The New Workforce: The pandemic accelerated the shift toward remote work, leading to a surge in gig and freelance opportunities. According to a 2024 report by McKinsey, nearly 50% of U.S. workers are now engaged in some form of gig work.

Financial Opportunities: This shift offers opportunities for increased income, but it also presents challenges, such as the lack of benefits that traditional employment provides.

Strategies for Gig Workers:

Income Diversification: Consider multiple income streams to mitigate the risk of fluctuations in gig work. For example, a graphic designer might freelance while also selling digital products online.

Financial Planning: Develop a budget that accounts for variable income. Setting aside a percentage of each paycheck for taxes and retirement savings is essential.

5. Technological Advancements

Fintech Revolution: The financial technology sector has exploded, with apps and platforms designed to simplify budgeting, saving, and investing. For instance, robo-advisors like Betterment and Wealthfront offer automated investment management services.

The Impact of AI: Artificial intelligence is enhancing personal finance management by providing personalised insights and recommendations based on spending habits.

Staying Informed:

Explore New Tools: Regularly review and experiment with new budgeting and investment apps. Many offer free trials, allowing you to find the best fit for your needs.

Continuous Learning: Consider online courses or webinars on personal finance topics to stay updated on the latest trends and tools.

Implications for Personal Finance

Understanding these trends is essential for adapting your financial strategies. Here are some actionable insights to consider:

Budgeting with Inflation in Mind: Adjust your budget categories to reflect rising costs. This might involve increasing your grocery budget or allocating more for utilities.

Embracing Digital Currency: If you're interested in cryptocurrencies, allocate a small, manageable portion of your investments to this asset class while diversifying your portfolio.

Making Ethical Choices: Create a checklist of brands that align with your values. This can guide your purchasing decisions and help you support businesses that contribute positively to society.

Navigating the Gig Economy: Build a financial cushion to manage income variability, especially if you rely on gig work. This could include establishing a separate savings account for taxes and irregular expenses.

Leveraging Technology: Take advantage of financial apps to track your expenses, set savings goals, and manage investments. Regularly assess your financial health using these tools.

Chapter 2: Assessing Your Financial Health

Understanding your current financial situation is crucial for effective money management. This chapter will guide you through a comprehensive assessment of your financial health, helping you identify areas for improvement and set realistic financial goals for 2025.

Understanding Your Financial Health

1. Net Worth Calculation

What is Net Worth?: Your net worth is the difference between your total assets and total liabilities. It provides a clear snapshot of your financial health and is a key indicator of your financial progress over time.

How to Calculate:
Assets: List everything you own that has value, including:

Real Estate: Market value of your home and any rental properties.

Vehicles: Current market value of cars, motorcycles, etc.

Cash and Cash Equivalents: Savings accounts, checking accounts, and cash on hand.
Investments: Stocks, bonds, retirement accounts, and any other investments.

Personal Property: Valuable items like jewellery, art, or collectibles.

Liabilities: List all debts you owe, including:

Mortgages: Outstanding balance on your home loan.
Student Loans: Total amount owed for education.
Credit Card Debt: Current balances on credit cards.
Personal Loans: Any other loans, such as car loans or personal lines of credit.

Example Calculation:
Assets:
Home: $300,000
Car: $20,000
Savings: $50,000
Investments: $30,000
Total Assets: $400,000

Liabilities:
Mortgage: $200,000
Student Loans: $15,000
Credit Card Debt: $5,000
Total Liabilities: $220,000
Net Worth:
$\{Net\ Worth\} = 400{,}000 - 220{,}000 = 180{,}000.$

2. Income and Expense Assessment

Tracking Income: Document all sources of income, including.

Primary Employment: Salary or wages from your job.

Side Hustles: Income from freelance work, gig jobs, or part-time employment.

Passive Income: Earnings from investments, rental properties, or royalties.

Analysing Expenses: Categorise your monthly expenses into fixed and variable.

Fixed Expenses: Consistent monthly costs, such as rent, mortgage, insurance, and subscriptions.

Variable Expenses: Fluctuating costs, including groceries, dining out, entertainment, and travel.

Example:
Monthly Income: $5,000
Fixed Expenses: $2,500 (rent, utilities, insurance)
Variable Expenses: $1,500 (groceries, dining out, entertainment)
Total Expenses: $4,000
Surplus: $1,000 (Income - Expenses)

3. Understanding Debt Levels

Types of Debt: Differentiate between good debt and bad debt:

Good Debt: Debt that can enhance your future earning potential (e.g., student loans, mortgages).

Bad Debt: Debt that incurs high-interest rates and does not contribute to wealth (e.g., credit card debt).

Debt-to-Income Ratio: This ratio measures your monthly debt payments against your monthly gross income. A lower ratio indicates better financial health.

Healthy Ratios: A debt-to-income ratio below 36% is generally considered healthy, while ratios above this can indicate potential financial stress.

4. Emergency Fund Assessment

What is an Emergency Fund?: An emergency fund is a savings buffer that can cover unexpected expenses, such as medical bills, car repairs, or job loss.

How Much to Save: Financial experts typically recommend saving three to six months' worth of living expenses.

Building Your Fund: Start by setting a goal and contributing a fixed amount monthly. For example, if your monthly expenses are $3,000, aim for an emergency fund of $9,000 to $18,000.

Setting Realistic Financial Goals for 2025

1. Defining SMART Goals

Specific: Clearly define what you want to achieve. Instead of saying, "I want to save money," specify, "I want to save $5,000 for a vacation."

Measurable: Include quantifiable indicators. For example, "I will save $500 each month."

Achievable: Set realistic goals based on your current financial situation. Consider your income, expenses, and any obligations.

Relevant: Ensure your goals align with your broader financial objectives. For example, saving for a home down payment aligns with long-term wealth building.

Time-bound: Set a deadline for achieving your goals. For example, "I want to save $5,000 by December 2025."

2. Types of Financial Goals

Short-Term Goals (within 1 year):
Build an emergency fund.
Pay off credit card debt.
Save for a specific purchase (e.g., new appliance).

- Medium-Term Goals (1 to 5 years):
  Save for a home down payment.
  Fund a child's education.
  Build a travel fund for a significant trip.

- Long-Term Goals (5+ years):
  Save for retirement.

Achieve financial independence.
Invest in a rental property.

3. Creating an Action Plan

Prioritise Goals: Determine which goals are most important and allocate resources accordingly. Consider using a priority matrix to visualise which goals provide the most value.

Budgeting for Goals: Incorporate your goals into your monthly budget. Identify areas where you can cut back to free up funds for your goals.

Example: To save $5,000 for a vacation in one year, you'll need to save approximately $417 each month. You might adjust your budget by reducing dining out or entertainment expenses.

4. Monitoring Progress

Regular Check-ins: Schedule monthly or quarterly reviews of your financial situation and progress toward your goals. Adjust your strategies as needed based on your progress.

Celebrate Milestones: Acknowledge and celebrate small victories along the way. For instance, treat yourself to a small reward when you reach 25% of your savings goal.

5. Using Technology to Track Goals

Budgeting Apps: Consider using budgeting apps like YNAB or Mint to track your progress. Many of these tools allow you to set savings goals and monitor your spending in real-time.

Spreadsheets: If you prefer a more hands-on approach, create a spreadsheet to track your savings goals, expenses, and net worth over time.

Chapter 3: Crafting a Flexible Budget

Creating a budget is one of the most effective ways to take control of your finances. A well-structured budget not only helps you manage your expenses but also allows for flexibility to adapt to changing circumstances. This chapter will guide you through the steps of crafting a flexible budget that aligns with your financial goals for 2025.

Understanding the Basics of Budgeting

1. What is a Budget?

A budget is a financial plan that outlines expected income and expenses over a specific period. It helps you allocate resources effectively to meet your financial goals.

Budgets can be categorised into various types:

- Zero-Based Budgeting: Every dollar is allocated to specific expenses or savings, ensuring that total income minus total expenditures equals zero.

- 50/30/20 Rule: This popular budgeting method suggests allocating 50% of your income to needs, 30% to wants, and 20% to savings and debt repayment.

2. Benefits of Budgeting

Financial Awareness: A budget helps you understand where your money is going, enabling informed spending decisions.

Goal Achievement: By allocating funds toward specific goals, you can track your progress and stay motivated.

Stress Reduction: Knowing you have a plan for your finances can reduce anxiety and help you feel more in control.

Steps to Create a Flexible Budget

1. Gather Financial Information

- Income Sources: Collect information on all income sources, including salaries, freelance work, investments, and any side hustles.

- Expense Records: Gather data on your monthly expenses from bank statements, receipts, and previous budgets. Categorise these into fixed and variable expenses.

2. Categorise Your Expenses

- Fixed Expenses: These are regular monthly payments that do not change significantly (e.g., rent/mortgage, insurance, car payments).

- Variable Expenses: These fluctuate each month (e.g., groceries, entertainment, dining out).

- Discretionary Spending: Identify areas where you can cut back if necessary, such as subscriptions, eating out, or entertainment.

3. Set Financial Goals

- Define short-term, medium-term, and long-term goals. Determine how much you want to save for each goal and allocate funds in your budget accordingly.

- For example, if you want to save for a vacation costing $3,000 within a year, you would need to allocate $250 monthly.

4. Create the Budget

- Template: Use a budgeting template or software to organise your income and expenses. Include sections for each category, and be sure to differentiate between fixed and variable expenses.

- Example Budget Template:

Category	Monthly Income	Monthly Expenses
Salary	$4,500	
Freelance Income	$500	
Total Income	**$5,000**	**$4,200**
Rent		$1,200
Utilities		$200

Groceries	$400
Transportation	$300
Entertainment	$300
Savings	$500
Miscellaneous	$300
Total Expenses	**$4,200**
Surplus/Deficit	**$800**

5. Implement Flexibility

- Adjust as Needed: Life is unpredictable. Your budget should be a living document that adapts to changes in income or expenses. For example, if you receive a bonus, consider allocating a portion to savings or debt repayment.

- Review Regularly: Schedule monthly reviews to assess your budget. Are you staying on track? Do you need to adjust your spending in certain categories? This adaptability is key to a flexible budget.

6. Use Technology for Budgeting

- Budgeting Apps: Consider apps like Mint, YNAB, or Personal Capital, which can automate tracking and provide insights into your spending habits.

   - Spreadsheets: If you prefer a hands-on approach, create a budget spreadsheet in Excel or Google Sheets. This allows for easy customization and updates.

Tips for Sticking to Your Budget

1. Track Your Spending
   - Use your chosen budgeting tool to monitor spending in real-time. This will help you stay within your budget and make adjustments as necessary.

2. Set Up Alerts and Reminders
   - Many budgeting apps allow you to set up alerts for when you approach your spending limits in certain categories. This can help prevent overspending.

3. Involve Your Family or Partner
   - If you share finances with others, involve them in the budgeting process. This creates transparency and accountability, making it easier to stick to the budget as a team.

4. Reward Yourself

- Set aside a small percentage of your budget for discretionary spending or rewards. For instance, if you stay under budget for three consecutive months, treat yourself to a small indulgence.

5. Be Patient and Flexible
  - Adjusting to a new budgeting system takes time. Be patient with yourself, and don't be afraid to make changes as necessary. Flexibility is vital to maintaining a budget that works for you.

Chapter 4: Building Smart Spending Habits

Developing smart spending habits is crucial for financial success. The way you manage your expenditures can significantly impact your ability to save, invest, and achieve your financial goals. This chapter will guide you through practical strategies for cultivating smart spending habits that align with your budget.

Understanding Your Spending Triggers

1. Identify Emotional Spending

   - What is Emotional Spending?: Emotional spending occurs when purchases are driven by feelings rather than needs. Common triggers include stress, boredom, or happiness.

   - Self-Reflection: Keep a journal to track your spending habits. Write down what you bought, how much you spent, and your emotional state at the time. This can help identify patterns.

   - Example: If you notice that you tend to shop online when feeling stressed, you can develop alternative coping strategies, such as exercising or meditating.

2. Recognize Environmental Triggers

   - Influence of Surroundings: Your environment can influence your spending habits. For instance, if you frequently visit cafes with friends, you may be tempted to overspend on coffee and snacks.

   - Modify Your Environment: Change your surroundings to minimise triggers. If dining out is a temptation, consider hosting potlucks or cooking with friends at home.

Strategies for Smart Spending

1. Create a Shopping List
   - Plan Ahead: Before shopping, create a detailed list of what you need. This helps prevent impulse purchases and keeps you focused on essentials.

- Stick to the List: Only buy items on your list. If you see something else you want, note it down for later consideration instead of purchasing it immediately.

2. Implement the 24-Hour Rule

  - Delay Impulse Purchases: If you find something you want to buy but hadn't planned for, wait 24 hours before making the purchase. This cooling-off period can help you determine if the item is truly necessary.

  - Example: If you see a pair of shoes online, take a day to think about whether you really need them or if they will simply add clutter to your closet.

3. Use Cash for Discretionary Spending

   Set a Cash Budget: Withdraw a set amount of cash each month for discretionary spending (e.g., dining out, entertainment). Once the cash is gone, resist the urge to overspend.

  - Psychological Impact: Using cash can create a more tangible sense of spending compared to credit cards, making it easier to stick to your budget.

4. Leverage Technology for Discounts

- Apps and Websites: Use apps like Honey or Rakuten to find discounts and cashback offers when shopping online. These tools can help you save money and make informed purchases.

- Sign Up for Newsletters: Subscribe to newsletters from your favourite retailers to receive exclusive discounts and promotions.

5. Evaluate Subscription Services

- Assess Necessity: Review all subscription services (e.g., streaming services, magazines, gym memberships) to determine which ones you actually use and enjoy. Cancel those that are underused.

- Consolidate Services: Consider bundling subscriptions or choosing multi-use services to save money.

Mindful Spending Practices

1. Practice Gratitude
- Focus on What You Have: Regularly take time to reflect on and appreciate what you already own. This can help reduce the desire to acquire more stuff.

- Gratitude Journaling: Keep a gratitude journal where you write down things you appreciate in your life. This can shift your focus away from wanting more material possessions.

2. Think Long-Term

- Invest in Quality: When making purchases, consider the long-term value. Opt for higher-quality items that may cost more upfront but will last longer and save money over time.

- Example: Investing in a durable pair of shoes may seem expensive, but if they last several years, they can be more cost-effective than buying cheaper shoes that wear out quickly.

3. Set Up a "Want" Fund

- Allocate Funds for Wants: Create a separate budget category for discretionary spending. This fund allows you to indulge your desires without guilt, as long as it fits within your budget.

- Example: If you set aside $100 per month for "wants," you can use this fund for non-essential purchases guilt-free, knowing you've planned for it.

Review and Adjust Your Spending Habits

1. Monthly Spending Review
   - Track Your Expenses: At the end of each month, review your spending against your budget. Identify areas where you may have overspent and reflect on the reasons behind those choices.

   - Adjust as Needed: If certain categories consistently exceed your budget, consider adjusting your budget or finding ways to reduce spending in those areas.

2. Celebrate Successes
   - Acknowledge Achievements: Celebrate when you stick to your budget or successfully reduce spending in a specific category. Positive reinforcement can help motivate you to maintain smart spending habits.

3. Stay Flexible
   - Adapt Your Strategies: Life circumstances change, and so may your financial priorities. Be open to adjusting your spending habits and budget as needed to stay aligned with your goals.

Chapter 5: The Importance of Saving and Investing

Saving and investing are fundamental components of financial health that can help you achieve your financial goals and secure your future. This chapter will explore the significance of both saving and investing, the different types of savings and investment vehicles, and strategies to grow your wealth effectively.

Understanding the Importance of Saving

1. Establishing an Emergency Fund
   - What is an Emergency Fund?: An emergency fund is a savings buffer designed to cover unexpected expenses, such as medical bills, car repairs, or job loss.

   - Recommended Amount: Financial experts recommend saving three to six months' worth of living expenses. For example, if your monthly expenses total $3,000, aim for an emergency fund of $9,000 to $18,000.

- Building Your Fund: Start small and contribute regularly. Set a goal to contribute a specific amount each month until you reach your target.

2. Saving for Short-Term Goals

- Examples of Short-Term Goals: These might include saving for a vacation, a new car, or home repairs. Short-term goals typically have a timeline of one to five years.

- High-Interest Savings Accounts: Consider using high-yield savings accounts or money market accounts to save for short-term goals. These accounts often offer higher interest rates than traditional savings accounts, allowing your money to grow while remaining accessible.

3. Retirement Savings

- Why Save for Retirement?: The earlier you start saving for retirement, the more time your money has to grow through compound interest. This is crucial for ensuring financial security in your later years.

- Retirement Accounts:

- 401(k): Employer-sponsored retirement plans that often include matching contributions. Aim to contribute enough to take full advantage of any employer match.

- IRA: Individual Retirement Accounts (Traditional or Roth) offer tax advantages for retirement savings. Explore which type aligns best with your financial situation.

The Basics of Investing

1. What is Investing?
   - Investing involves allocating money into assets with the expectation of generating a return over time. This can include stocks, bonds, real estate, and mutual funds.

   - Difference Between Saving and Investing: While saving is about preserving capital for short-term needs, investing aims to grow wealth over the long term.

2. Understanding Risk and Return
   - Risk Tolerance: Your risk tolerance is your ability and willingness to endure fluctuations in the value of your investments. Assess your comfort level with risk before investing.
   - Risk vs. Reward: Generally, higher potential returns come with higher risk. For example, stocks have historically provided higher returns than bonds but are also more volatile.

3. Types of Investment Vehicles

- Stocks: Shares of ownership in a company. Stocks can provide high returns but also come with higher risk.

- Bonds: Debt securities issued by corporations or governments. Bonds are generally considered safer than stocks but typically offer lower returns.

- Mutual Funds and ETFs: These funds pool money from multiple investors to purchase a diversified portfolio of stocks or bonds. They provide an easy way to diversify your investments without having to buy individual securities.

- Real Estate: Investing in property can provide rental income and potential appreciation in value over time, although it requires a larger initial investment and can involve ongoing costs.

Strategies for Saving and Investing

1. Automate Your Savings
- Set Up Automatic Transfers: Automate transfers from your checking account to your savings or investment accounts. This "pay yourself first" approach ensures you consistently save a portion of your income without having to think about it.

- Example: If you receive a monthly paycheck, set up an automatic transfer to your emergency fund or retirement account on payday.

2. Diversify Your Investments
- Why Diversification Matters: Diversification helps reduce risk by spreading investments across various asset classes. This way, if one investment performs poorly, others may perform well and balance your portfolio.

- Portfolio Allocation: Consider a balanced portfolio that reflects your risk tolerance and investment goals. For example, a younger investor might have a higher percentage of stocks, while someone closer to retirement may prefer bonds.

3. Regularly Review and Adjust Your Portfolio

- Monitor Performance: Regularly review your investment portfolio to ensure it aligns with your financial goals and risk tolerance. Adjust your asset allocation as needed based on market conditions and life changes.

- Rebalancing: If one asset class significantly outperforms others, consider rebalancing your portfolio to maintain your desired asset allocation.

4. Educate Yourself Continuously

   - Stay Informed: Keep learning about personal finance and investment strategies. Read books, attend seminars, and follow reputable financial news sources.

   - Join Investment Clubs: Consider joining local or online investment clubs where you can share insights and learn from others.

Chapter 6: Mastering Debt Management

Debt can be a significant barrier to financial stability and success. However, with effective management strategies, you can take control of your debt and work towards financial freedom. This chapter will explore various types of debt, strategies for paying off debt, and tips for maintaining a healthy financial future.

Understanding Different Types of Debt

1. Good Debt vs. Bad Debt

   - Good Debt: This type of debt is considered an investment in your future. Examples include student loans, mortgages, and business loans. These debts can lead to increased earning potential or asset accumulation.

   - Bad Debt: High-interest debt that does not contribute to your financial growth. This includes credit card debt and personal loans used for non-essential purchases. Bad debt can negatively impact your financial health.

2. Common Types of Debt

- Credit Card Debt: Often incurs high-interest rates and can quickly accumulate if not managed properly.

- Student Loans: Can be a necessary investment in education but may become burdensome if repayment plans are not well-structured.

- Mortgages: Typically lower interest rates compared to other debts, but a significant long-term commitment.

- Personal Loans: Can be used for various purposes, but often come with higher interest rates than mortgages.

Strategies for Paying Off Debt

1. Create a Debt Inventory

- List All Debts: Write down all your debts, including the total amount owed, interest rates, and minimum monthly payments. This will give you a clear picture of what you're dealing with.

- Example Debt Inventory:

Creditor	Total Owed	Interest Rate	Minimum Payment
Credit Card 1	$3,000	18%	$100
Student Loan	$15,000	4%	$150
Car Loan	$8,000	6%	$200
Personal Loan	$5,000	12%	$120

2. Choose a Debt Repayment Strategy

   - Snowball Method: Focus on paying off the smallest debt first while making minimum payments on larger debts. Once the smallest debt is paid off, move to the next smallest. This method can provide psychological wins and motivation to continue.

   - Avalanche Method: Pay off debts with the highest interest rates first, which minimises the total interest paid over time. This method is often more cost-effective in the long run.

   - Example: If you choose the snowball method, you would start with Credit Card 1, while making minimum payments on the other debts.

3. Make Extra Payments

- Pay More Than the Minimum: Whenever possible, pay more than the minimum required on your debts. This can significantly reduce the total interest paid and shorten the repayment period.

- Use Windfalls Wisely: Allocate bonuses, tax refunds, or any unexpected financial windfalls toward debt repayment to accelerate your progress.

4. Negotiate Lower Interest Rates

- Contact Your Creditors: Reach out to your creditors to negotiate lower interest rates. A good payment history may give you leverage in these discussions.

- Consolidation Options: Consider consolidating high-interest debts into a lower-interest loan or balance transfer credit card. This can simplify payments and reduce interest costs.

5. Set Up a Budget for Debt Repayment

- Allocate Funds: Create a budget that prioritises debt repayment. Ensure that you allocate a specific amount each month towards your debt.

- Track Progress: Regularly review your budget and track your progress in paying off debt. Celebrate milestones to stay motivated.

Maintaining a Healthy Financial Future

1. Avoid Accumulating More Debt

- Limit Credit Card Use: Use credit cards only for necessary purchases and pay off the balance in full each month to avoid interest charges.

- Build an Emergency Fund: Having an emergency fund can prevent reliance on credit for unexpected expenses.

2. Educate Yourself About Personal Finance

- Continuous Learning: Read books, attend workshops, or take online courses about personal finance, budgeting, and debt management to improve your financial literacy.

- Seek Professional Advice: If you're struggling with debt, consider consulting a financial advisor or credit counsellor for personalised guidance.

3. Monitor Your Credit Score

- Regularly Check Your Credit Report: Monitor your credit score and report for accuracy. Address any discrepancies promptly to maintain a healthy credit profile.
- Understand Credit Utilisation: Aim to keep your credit utilisation ratio (the amount of credit you're using compared to your total credit limit) below 30%. This positively impacts your credit score.

Chapter 7: The Importance of Insurance

Insurance is a critical component of a comprehensive financial plan. It provides financial protection against unexpected events that could otherwise lead to significant financial loss. This chapter will explore the various types of insurance, their importance, and how to choose the right coverage for your needs.

Understanding the Role of Insurance

1. What is Insurance?

   - Insurance is a financial product that provides compensation for specific losses in exchange for regular premium payments. It helps protect you from financial burdens caused by unforeseen events.

2. Why is Insurance Important?

- Risk Management: Insurance mitigates the financial impact of risks such as accidents, illnesses, and property damage. It allows you to manage potential losses without crippling your finances.

- Peace of Mind: Knowing you have coverage can alleviate anxiety regarding unexpected events, allowing you to focus on other aspects of your life.

- Asset Protection: Insurance helps protect your assets, ensuring that you can recover financially from losses and continue to maintain your standard of living.

Types of Insurance to Consider

1. Health Insurance

- What it Covers: Health insurance helps pay for medical expenses, including doctor visits, hospital stays, prescription medications, and preventive care.

- Choosing a Plan: Assess your healthcare needs and budget when selecting a health insurance plan. Consider factors such as premiums, deductibles, and coverage networks.

2. Life Insurance

   - Purpose: Life insurance provides financial support to your beneficiaries in the event of your death. It can help cover living expenses, debts, and future financial goals (e.g., children's education).

   - Types of Life Insurance:
      - Term Life Insurance: Provides coverage for a specified period (e.g., 10, 20, or 30 years). It is generally more affordable and suitable for temporary needs.

      - Whole Life Insurance: Offers lifelong coverage and includes a cash value component that grows over time. It tends to be more expensive but can serve as a long-term investment.

3. Auto Insurance

   - What it Covers: Auto insurance protects you from financial loss resulting from accidents, theft, or damage to your vehicle.

   - Types of Coverage:

      - Liability Coverage: Covers damages to other people or property in an accident you cause.

- Collision Coverage: Pays for damage to your vehicle in an accident, regardless of fault.
   - Comprehensive Coverage: Covers non-collision-related incidents (e.g., theft, vandalism, natural disasters).

4. Homeowners or Renters Insurance
   - Homeowners Insurance: Protects your home and personal belongings against damage or loss due to events like fire, theft, or natural disasters. It also provides liability coverage in case someone is injured on your property.

   - Renters Insurance: Covers personal belongings in a rented property and provides liability protection. It is often more affordable than homeowners insurance.

5. Disability Insurance
   - Purpose: Disability insurance provides income replacement if you become unable to work due to illness or injury. It helps ensure you can meet your financial obligations during a period of disability.

   -Types:
   - Short-Term Disability Insurance: Provides coverage for a limited period (usually up to six months).
   - Long-Term Disability Insurance: Offers coverage for extended periods, potentially until retirement age.

6. Umbrella Insurance

- What it Covers: Umbrella insurance provides additional liability coverage beyond the limits of your existing policies (e.g., auto, homeowners). It protects you from large claims and lawsuits.

- Importance: This type of insurance is particularly valuable if you have significant assets to protect or if you are at higher risk of being sued.

Choosing the Right Insurance Coverage

1. Assess Your Needs

- Evaluate your financial situation, lifestyle, and risk exposure to determine the types and amounts of insurance coverage you need. Consider factors such as dependents, assets, and potential liabilities.

2. Compare Policies
- Research multiple insurance providers and compare their policies. Look for coverage options, premiums, deductibles, and customer reviews. Online comparison tools can facilitate this process.

3. Consider Bundling Policies

- Many insurance companies offer discounts for bundling multiple types of insurance (e.g., auto and homeowners). This can lead to significant savings while simplifying your insurance management.

4. Regularly Review Your Coverage
   - Your insurance needs may change over time due to life events such as marriage, the birth of a child, or changes in income. Regularly review your policies to ensure your coverage remains adequate.

5. Consult an Insurance Professional
   - If you're unsure about your insurance needs or how to choose the right policies, consider consulting an insurance agent or financial advisor. They can provide personalised guidance based on your circumstances.

Chapter 8: The Importance of Estate Planning

Estate planning is a crucial aspect of financial management that ensures your wishes are fulfilled after your passing and protects your loved ones. This chapter will explore the fundamentals of estate planning, key documents involved, and strategies to effectively plan for your future.

Understanding Estate Planning

1. What is Estate Planning?
   - Estate planning involves arranging for the management and distribution of your assets after your death. It ensures that your wishes regarding your property, finances, and healthcare are honoured and can minimise the burdens on your loved ones.

2. Why is Estate Planning Important?

- Asset Protection: Proper estate planning helps protect your assets and ensures they are distributed according to your wishes.

- Minimising Taxes: A well-structured estate plan can reduce estate taxes and other financial burdens on your heirs.

- Avoiding Probate: Planning ahead can help your estate avoid the lengthy and costly probate process, allowing for quicker access to your assets for your beneficiaries.

- Healthcare Decisions: Estate planning includes provisions for healthcare decisions in case you become incapacitated, ensuring your medical preferences are honoured.

Key Components of an Estate Plan

1. Wil

- What is a Will?: A will is a legal document that outlines how your assets will be distributed after your death. It also allows you to name guardians for minor children.

- Creating a Will: Work with an attorney or use reputable online services to ensure your will complies with state laws. Regularly review and update it as your circumstances change.

2. Trusts

- What is a Trust?: A trust is a legal arrangement that allows a third party (the trustee) to hold assets on behalf of beneficiaries. Trusts can help manage assets during your lifetime and after your death.

Types of Trusts

- Revocable Living Trust: Allows you to maintain control over your assets while alive and facilitates easier transfer upon death without going through probate.

- Irrevocable Trust: Once established, this trust cannot be altered. It can provide tax benefits and protect assets from creditors.

3. Power of Attorney (POA)

- What is POA?: A power of attorney is a legal document that grants someone the authority to make decisions on your behalf if you become incapacitated. This can include financial, legal, or medical decisions.

- Choosing an Agent: Select a trusted individual who understands your values and wishes. Discuss your intentions openly to ensure they are prepared for this responsibility.

4. Health Care Proxy and Living Will

- Health Care Proxy: This document designates someone to make medical decisions on your behalf if you are unable to do so.

- Living Will: A living will outlines your preferences for medical treatment and end-of-life care, ensuring your wishes are followed in critical situations.

5. Beneficiary Designations

- Review Designations: Ensure that your beneficiary designations on accounts such as life insurance, retirement accounts, and bank accounts are up to date. These designations override wills and trusts, so it's crucial to keep them current.

Strategies for Effective Estate Planning

1. Start Early

- Don't Delay: Estate planning is not just for the wealthy or elderly. Start planning early to ensure your wishes are documented and to avoid potential complications in the future.

2. Regularly Review Your Plan
   - Life Changes: Major life events such as marriage, divorce, the birth of children, or significant financial changes should prompt a review of your estate plan. Update documents as needed to reflect your current situation.

3. Communicate Your Wishes
   - Discuss with Family: Openly communicate your estate planning decisions with your family and loved ones. This can help prevent misunderstandings and conflicts after your passing.

4. Work with Professionals
   - Seek Expert Guidance: Consider working with estate planning attorneys, financial advisors, and tax professionals to ensure your plan is comprehensive and legally sound.

5. Consider Charitable Giving
   - Incorporate Philanthropy: If you wish to leave a legacy, consider including charitable donations in your estate plan. This can provide tax benefits

and fulfil your desire to support causes you care about.

Chapter 9: The Importance of Continuous Financial Education

In an ever-evolving financial landscape, continuous education is essential for making informed decisions and achieving long-term financial success. This chapter will explore the importance of financial literacy, resources for education, and strategies to stay informed about personal finance.

Understanding Financial Literacy

1. What is Financial Literacy?
   - Financial literacy refers to the ability to understand and effectively use various financial skills, including budgeting, investing, borrowing, and managing debt. It equips individuals with the knowledge to make informed financial decisions.

2. Why is Financial Literacy Important?

- Empowerment: Being financially literate empowers you to take control of your finances, make informed decisions, and achieve your financial goals.

- Avoiding Debt: Understanding financial concepts helps you avoid common pitfalls, such as excessive debt and poor investment choices.

- Planning for the Future: Financial literacy allows you to plan for significant life events, such as retirement, homeownership, and education expenses.

Resources for Financial Education

1. Books

- Personal Finance Books: There are numerous books available that cover a wide range of financial topics, from budgeting to investing. Some popular titles include:

2. Online Courses and Webinars

- Educational Platforms: Websites like Coursera, Udemy, and Khan Academy offer courses on personal finance, investing, and financial planning. Many are free or low-cost and provide valuable knowledge.

- Webinars: Financial institutions, non-profits, and financial advisors often host webinars on various topics. These can be a great way to learn from experts.

3. Podcasts and Blogs
   - Podcasts: Financial podcasts can provide insights and tips from experienced professionals. Some popular options include:
     - "The Dave Ramsey Show"
     - "The BiggerPockets Podcast"
     - "Smart Passive Income" by Pat Flynn
   - Blogs: Follow reputable financial blogs to stay updated on the latest trends, tips, and strategies in personal finance.

4. Financial News and Publications
   - Stay Informed: Regularly read financial news from sources like Bloomberg, The Wall Street Journal, or CNBC. This helps you stay informed about market trends and economic changes that may impact your finances.

5. Financial Advisors
   - Professional Guidance: Consider working with a certified financial planner or advisor who can provide personalised advice tailored to your financial situation and goals.

Strategies for Continuous Learning

1. Set Financial Goals

- Learning Objectives: Establish specific financial learning goals, such as improving your investment knowledge or understanding retirement planning. This will give you direction in your education journey.

2. Create a Learning Schedule
   - Allocate Time: Dedicate regular time each week or month for financial education. Consistency will help reinforce your learning and keep you engaged.

3. Join Financial Communities
   - Networking: Engage with online forums, social media groups, or local clubs focused on personal finance. Sharing experiences and insights with others can enhance your understanding and motivation.

4. Apply What You Learn
   - Practical Application: Implement new knowledge in your financial life. For example, if you learn about investment strategies, consider applying them to your portfolio. Real-world application reinforces learning.

5. Stay Open to Change
   - Adaptability: The financial landscape is constantly changing. Stay open to new ideas and be willing to adjust your strategies as you learn more and gain experience.

Chapter 10: Travel and Experience Budgeting

Travelling can be one of the most enriching experiences in life, but it requires careful planning and budgeting to ensure that it doesn't lead to financial strain. This chapter will explore strategies for budgeting for travel in 2025, balancing memorable experiences with financial responsibility.

Strategies for Planning and Budgeting for Travel

1. Set Clear Travel Goals
   - Define Your Travel Objectives: Determine what you want to achieve with your trip. Are you looking for adventure, relaxation, cultural experiences, or family bonding? Clear goals will guide your planning and budgeting.

   - Choose Destinations Wisely: Research potential destinations that align with your goals and budget.

Consider factors such as cost of living, travel restrictions, and seasonal variations in pricing.

2. Create a Travel Budget

- Estimate Total Costs: Break down your budget into categories such as transportation, accommodation, food, activities, and souvenirs. Research average costs for each category based on your chosen destination.

- Use a Budgeting Tool: Utilise budgeting apps or spreadsheets to track your travel expenses. This will help you stay organised and accountable.

3. Save in Advance

- Open a Dedicated Travel Fund: Create a separate savings account specifically for travel expenses. Automate transfers to this account from your main income to ensure consistent saving.

- Set a Savings Goal: Determine how much you need for your trip and set a timeline to reach that goal. Break it down into manageable monthly contributions.

4. Be Flexible with Travel Dates

- Off-Peak Travel: If possible, plan your trip during off-peak seasons to take advantage of lower prices on flights and accommodations. Flexibility can lead to significant savings.

- Use Fare Alerts: Sign up for fare alerts on flight comparison websites to catch deals on flights that fit your schedule.

5. Research and Compare Options
   - Accommodation Choices: Explore various lodging options, including hotels, hostels, vacation rentals, or even home exchanges. Compare prices and read reviews to find the best fit for your budget.

   - Transportation Alternatives: Consider public transportation, car rentals, or ride-sharing services. Research the most cost-effective ways to get around your destination.

6. Prioritise Experiences
   - Budget for Activities: Allocate funds for experiences that align with your travel goals. Whether it's a guided tour, a cooking class, or a local event, prioritise experiences that will enhance your trip.

   - Look for Free or Low-Cost Activities: Research free events, parks, and attractions in your destination. Many cities offer free walking tours or community events that can provide rich experiences without breaking the bank.

Balancing Experiences with Financial Responsibility

1. Make Trade-Offs
    - Evaluate Costs vs. Benefits: Consider what experiences are most important to you. If a particular activity is costly, weigh its value against other experiences you could have for less money.

    - Set Spending Limits: For discretionary spending like dining or entertainment, set daily or trip-wide limits to keep your budget in check.

2. Track Your Spending While Travelling

    - Daily Expense Tracking: Use apps or a simple notebook to track your daily spending. This helps you stay mindful of your budget and make adjustments as needed.

    - Reflect and Adjust: If you find you're overspending in one category, reassess your plans for the rest of the trip. Adjustments can help you stay within budget without sacrificing enjoyment.

3. Plan for the Unexpected
    - Include a Contingency Fund: Set aside a portion of your budget for unexpected expenses, such as medical

emergencies or last-minute changes in plans. This will provide peace of mind during your travels.

- Travel Insurance: Consider purchasing travel insurance to protect against unforeseen circumstances that could disrupt your trip or result in additional costs.

Chapter 11: Adapting to Economic Shifts

In a world marked by constant change, economic shifts can impact our financial stability and goals. This chapter will explore how to stay financially agile in uncertain times and prepare for potential economic challenges.

Staying Financially Agile in Uncertain Times

1. Monitor Economic Indicators

- Stay Informed: Regularly follow economic news and indicators, such as inflation rates, employment statistics, and consumer confidence. Understanding these factors can help you make informed financial decisions.

- Use Reliable Sources: Rely on reputable financial news outlets and economic reports to stay updated on shifts that could affect your finances.

2. Diversify Income Streams

- Explore Side Gigs: Consider developing additional sources of income, such as freelance work, consulting, or passive income streams like rental properties or investments.

- Invest in Skills: Continuously improve your skills and knowledge to enhance your employability. Online courses and certifications can make you more competitive in the job market.

3. Maintain an Emergency Fund

- Build Financial Resilience: Aim to save three to six months' worth of living expenses in an easily accessible account. This fund serves as a safety net during economic downturns or unexpected job loss.

- Regular Contributions: Treat your emergency fund as a priority, contributing to it regularly until you reach your target amount.

4. Reduce Unnecessary Expenses

- Review Your Budget: Conduct a thorough review of your monthly expenses to identify non-essential costs. Cut back on discretionary spending to increase your savings.

- Adopt a Minimalist Mindset: Focus on needs rather than wants. This mindset can help you make more intentional financial choices and prioritise savings.

Preparing for Potential Economic Challenges

1. Create a Flexible Financial Plan

- Set Short-Term and Long-Term Goals: Develop a financial plan that includes both immediate and future goals. Ensure your plan is adaptable to changing circumstances.

- Adjust as Necessary: Revisit and adjust your financial plan regularly based on changes in your personal situation or the economy.

2. Invest Wisely

- Diversify Your Investments: Spread your investments across different asset classes (stocks, bonds, real estate) to mitigate risk. A diversified portfolio can help weather economic fluctuations.

- Stay Informed About Market Trends: Keep abreast of market trends that may affect your investments, and be prepared to make adjustments as needed.

3. Consider Insurance Coverage

- Evaluate Your Policies: Ensure you have adequate insurance coverage (health, life, disability) to protect against unforeseen circumstances. This can provide financial security during tough times.

- Explore Policy Options: Regularly review your insurance policies to ensure they meet your changing needs and consider additional coverage as necessary.

4. Build a Strong Professional Network

- Networking Opportunities: Engage with professional organisations and attend industry events to expand your network. A strong network can provide support and opportunities during economic challenges.

- Seek Mentorship: Connect with mentors who can offer guidance and advice on navigating financial uncertainties and career transitions.

5. Stay Flexible and Open to Change

 - Embrace Adaptability: Be willing to pivot your plans and adjust your strategies as economic conditions evolve. Flexibility is key to thriving in uncertain times.

 - Cultivate a Growth Mindset: Approach challenges as opportunities for growth. Learning from setbacks can enhance your resilience and financial acumen.

Chapter 12: Resources for Financial Success

Achieving financial success requires not only knowledge and planning but also the right tools and support systems. This chapter will explore recommended tools, apps, and books for further learning, as well as strategies for building a network of financial support.

Recommended Tools, Apps, and Books for Further Learning

1. Financial Tools and Apps
   Budgeting Apps:

   - Mint: A comprehensive budgeting tool that tracks expenses, sets budgets, and provides insights into your spending habits.

- YNAB (You Need A Budget): A proactive budgeting app that helps you allocate every dollar and encourages mindful spending.

Investment Apps:

- Robinhood: A user-friendly platform for commission-free trading of stocks, ETFs, and cryptocurrencies.

- Acorns: An app that rounds up your purchases and invests the spare change in diversified portfolios.

- Savings and Goal-Tracking Apps:

- : Allows you to set savings goals and automate saving through customizable rules (e.g., round-up savings).

- Digit: An app that analyses your spending habits and automatically saves small amounts of money for you.

2. Recommended Book
   - Personal Finance Classics:

- "The Total Money Makeover" by Dave Ramsey: A practical guide to budgeting, saving, and getting out of debt.

- "Rich Dad Poor Dad" by Robert Kiyosaki: Offers insights into the mindset and financial education needed for wealth-building.

- Investing and Wealth Building:

- "The Intelligent Investor" by Benjamin Graham: A foundational text on value investing and understanding market behaviour.

- "The Simple Path to Wealth" by JL Collins: A straightforward approach to investing and achieving financial independence.

- Financial Psychology:
- "Your Money or Your Life" by Vicki Robin and Joe Dominguez: Explores the relationship between money and personal values, advocating for mindful financial choices.

3. Online Courses and Resources

- Coursera and Udemy: Offer a variety of courses on personal finance, investing, and financial literacy. Look for courses taught by reputable instructors or institutions.

- Khan Academy: Provides free resources on economics and personal finance, making complex topics accessible to everyone.

Building a Network of Financial Support

1. Engaging with Financial Communities

- Online Forums and Groups: Join platforms like Reddit (e.g., r/personalfinance) or Facebook groups focused on personal finance. These communities can provide support, advice, and shared experiences.

- Local Meetups: Look for local finance meetups or workshops in your area. Engaging with like-minded individuals can enhance your knowledge and provide inspiration.

2. Networking with Professionals

- Financial Advisors: Consider working with a certified financial planner who can provide personalised advice based on your financial situation and goals. Look for fiduciaries who prioritise your best interests.

- Mentorship: Seek mentors in your professional or personal life who have experience in finance or investing. Their guidance can be invaluable as you navigate your financial journey.

3. Accountability Partners

- Find a Buddy: Partner with a friend or family member who shares similar financial goals. Regularly check in with each other to discuss progress, challenges, and successes.

- Financial Support Groups: Consider joining or forming a financial support group where members can share resources, tips, and experiences in a structured environment.

4. Utilising Social Media

- Follow Financial Influencers: Engage with financial experts on platforms like Instagram, Twitter, or YouTube. Many provide valuable tips and insights that can enhance your knowledge.

- Participate in Online Discussions: Join Twitter chats or LinkedIn groups focused on finance to stay informed and connect with others in the field.

Conclusion

As we wrap up this journey through the intricacies of personal finance, it's important to reflect on the key insights shared throughout the chapters. The path to financial success requires a blend of knowledge, planning, discipline, and community support. Here's a recap of the essential themes we've explored:

Recap of Key Insights

1. Setting Clear Financial Goals: Establishing specific, measurable, and realistic goals is foundational to your financial journey. Whether short-term or long-term, clear goals provide direction and motivation.

2. Creating a Flexible Budget: A well-structured budget is your roadmap to financial health. Regularly tracking your income and expenses enables you to make informed decisions and adapt to changing circumstances.

3. Building Smart Spending Habits: Being mindful of your spending and distinguishing between needs and wants can lead to significant savings and more financial freedom.

4. Saving and Investing Wisely: Prioritising savings, particularly through an emergency fund, and understanding the basics of investing can help build wealth over time. Diversification and regular portfolio reviews are key strategies for successful investing.

5. Managing Debt Effectively: Developing a clear debt repayment strategy can help you regain control over your finances. Staying disciplined and avoiding unnecessary debt is crucial for long-term financial health.

6. The Role of Insurance and Estate Planning: Protecting your assets through appropriate insurance coverage and planning for the future with a comprehensive estate plan ensures peace of mind for you and your loved ones.

7. Continuous Financial Education: The financial landscape is ever-evolving. Committing to ongoing education through books, courses, and financial communities empowers you to stay informed and make sound decisions.

8. Adapting to Economic Shifts: Staying financially agile is essential in uncertain times. Building a diverse income stream, maintaining an emergency fund, and being adaptable can help you weather economic challenges.

9. Leveraging Resources and Networks: Utilising the right tools and building a supportive network can enhance your financial journey. Engaging with communities and seeking mentorship can provide invaluable insights and encouragement.

Encouragement for Readers to Take Charge of Their Financial Future

As you move forward, remember that taking charge of your financial future is a journey, not a destination. The insights and strategies outlined in this book are now tools for you to implement, adapt, and personalise according to your unique circumstances.

Embrace the power of knowledge and action. Start small, set a financial goal, create a budget, or begin an investment plan. Celebrate your progress, no matter how minor, and remain committed to your financial education.

Your financial future is in your hands. With determination, discipline, and the right resources, you can achieve the financial stability and independence you desire. Trust in your ability to make informed decisions and seek support when needed.

Here's to your journey toward financial empowerment and success!

www.ingramcontent.com/pod-product-compliance
Lightning Source LLC
Chambersburg PA
CBHW070401230526
45471CB00006B/2658